YEARS 4 & 5

MULTIPLICATION TABLES

Do you need to know the basics of multiplication tables? Let's learn about them together.

Parents and carers are encouraged to read the explanation and practice sections with their child.

Ann Baker

Illustrated by Janice Bowles

About this book

Each unit in this book begins with a brief **explanation** of a concept or a strategy. You are encouraged to read this explanation with your child and, where appropriate, to use everyday materials and examples to give meaning to the concepts.

We practise is a worked example for you and your child to discuss together, paying particular attention to the thinking processes required to understand the concept or apply the strategy.

You practise gives your child the opportunity to practise the concept or strategy. It also indicates how well your child understands the new material and often includes problem-solving questions to ensure that your child has mastered the concept or strategy.

If further support is required, you and your child's teacher can devise a plan to ensure that all the basic concepts are fully understood and consolidated.

The **Tests** at the end of the book are provided to check that the concepts are fully understood. Test 1 can be done after units 1–10 are completed and Test 2 when the book is finished.

Meet 'BOB' – Back Of the Book

At the end of each unit, BOB reminds your child to go to the Answers section at the back of the book.

Mathematical Content

This book has been designed to cover the concept of multiplication tables that your child will encounter in **Year 4** and **Year 5**. The units provide a comprehensive coverage of the following Key Topics from the **Australian Curriculum: Mathematics.**

Australian Curriculum : Mathematics

YEAR 4

Recall multiplication facts up to 10 × 10 and related division facts (ACMNA075)

Develop efficient mental and written strategies and use appropriate digital technologies for multiplication and division where there is no remainder (ACMNA076)

YEAR 5

Identify and describe factors and multiples of whole numbers and use them to solve problems (ACMNA098)

Solve problems involving multiplication of large numbers by one- or two-digit numbers using efficient mental, written strategies and appropriate digital technologies (ACMNA100)

Contents & Checklist

WRITING and TALKING ABOUT MULTIPLICATION TABLES

When two numbers are **multiplied**, we say the multiplication sign as **times**:

3 × 7   3 times 7

For **division**, we say the division sign as **divided by**:

21 ÷ 7   21 divided by 7

Strategies

Here are the **four main strategies** that will help you work out and then learn multiplication facts:

Turnarounds: use the multiplication facts that have the same numbers, but in a different order.

9 × 5   think 5 × 9 = 45 and then **turnaround** to get 9 × 5 = 45

Double double: you know your 2s facts, so for the 4s facts just **double** the 2s facts.

4 × 7   think 2 × 7 = 14 and then **double** the answer to get 4 × 7 = 28

Near 10s: you know your **10s facts**, so you can use them to work out other facts.

9 × 5   think 10 × 5 = 50 and then **subtract** 5 to get 9 × 5 = 45

Close-by facts: you can use the facts that you already know to work out facts that are **close-by**.

6 × 6   think 6 × 5 = 30 and then **add** 6 to get 6 × 6 = 36

There are also three special words associated with **multiplication** and **division** that you should know:

Product: the answer to a multiplication fact or question.

6 × 9 = 54

54 is the **product** of 6 and 9

Multiple: one number is a multiple of another number if it is the product of that number and some other number.

4 × 5 = 20

20 is a **multiple** of 4 because it is the **product** of 4 × 5.

Factor: a number that you multiply with another number to get the product.

5 × 4 = 20   5 and 4 are **factors** of **20**

Other factors of 20 are 2, 4, 5 and 10 and these are called the **proper factors** of 20.

1 is a **factor** of every number and every number is a factor of itself.

GAME CARD IDEAS

Cut out the game cards – they will last longer if they are laminated. Here are some games for you to try.

SNAP!

A game for 2–4 players. All of the cards are dealt to the players. Each player then takes it in turn to place a card in a central pile, face up. The first player to call 'Snap' if a matching multiplication fact is placed on top of a card, wins the pile. The player who finishes holding all of the cards is the winner.

Fish

Three cards are dealt to each player. On their turn, players put down a matching pair and pick up two replacement cards. If they cannot go, they can '**fish**' by asking the other players for a card that they need. For example, if a player holds 90, they ask, 'Do you have 9 × 10 or 10 × 9 please?'

If anyone has that card, then they must give it up and the other player says 'thank you'. If a player is unable to play, they may discard a card and replace it, ready for the next round.

The player with most matching pairs wins the game.

Note: The 'please' and 'thank you' are part of the traditional *Happy Families* game and can add an entertaining twist.

Memory

Each card is placed face down. On their turn, a player turns over two cards. If they are a matching pair of multiplication facts, then they keep that pair and play again. If not, then play passes to the next person. The person with most matching pairs is the winner.

NOTE: Games are meant to be fun and provide practice without stress. It is recommended that you stop playing while you are still having fun and then your child will want to play again another time. If your child needs assistance, help them out or suggest that they use the tables chart at the back of the book.

UNIT 1 MASTERING THE 5s FACTS

Notice the 0, 5, 0, 5 pattern in the 5s counting sequence:

0 5 10 15 20 25 30 35

40 45 50 55 60 ...

This pattern goes on forever and never changes, so you will always know if a number is in the 5s counting sequence.

Here are the 5s facts:

5 × 0 = 0
5 × 1 = 5
5 × 2 = 10
5 × 3 = 15
5 × 4 = 20
5 × 5 = 25
5 × 6 = 30
5 × 7 = 35
5 × 8 = 40
5 × 9 = 45
5 × 10 = 50

Did you notice that when you multiply an **odd number** by 5 the answer always ends with a 5? And when you multiply an **even number** by 5 the answer always ends in 0?

Telling the time has a 5s pattern too. The hours on a clock face go up by 1, but the minutes go up by 5.

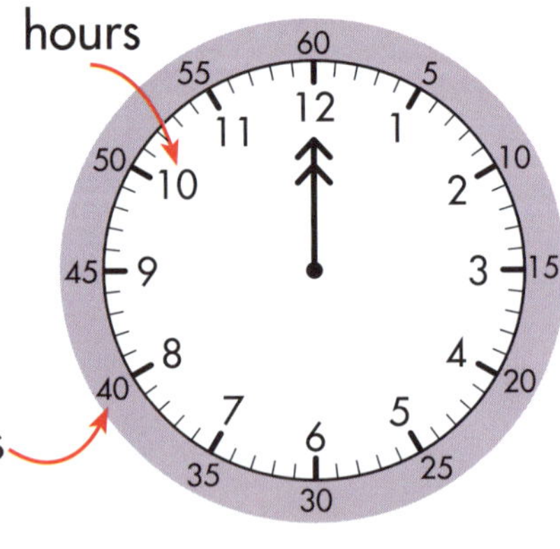

We practise

Complete these 5s facts. Tick the facts that have an odd number as the answer.

5 × 3 = 15 ✓
5 × 4 = 20
5 × 2 = 10
7 × 5 = 35 ✓
9 × 5 = 45 ✓

Complete these 5s facts. Tick the facts that have an even number as the answer.

5 × 6 = 30 ✓
5 × 7 = 35
5 × 8 = 40 ✓
4 × 5 = 20 ✓
11 × 5 = 55

You practise

Complete these 5s facts.
Tick the facts that have an odd number as the answer.

$5 \times 9 =$ _____

$5 \times 4 =$ _____

$5 \times 11 =$ _____

$5 \times 7 =$ _____

$5 \times 2 =$ _____

6 $5 \times 1 =$ _____

7 $5 \times 12 =$ _____

8 $3 \times 5 =$ _____

9 $10 \times 5 =$ _____

$5 \times 5 =$ _____

Remember, an odd number multiplied by 5 always ends with a 5.

Before completing each fact, tick the facts that will have an answer ending with a zero.

$5 \times 2 =$ _____

$5 \times 3 =$ _____

$5 \times 7 =$ _____

$5 \times 12 =$ _____

$5 \times 10 =$ _____

$5 \times 5 =$ _____

17 $5 \times 6 =$ _____

18 $8 \times 5 =$ _____

19 $1 \times 5 =$ _____

20 $4 \times 5 =$ _____

Remember, an even number multiplied by 5 always ends with a zero.

BOB time!

WORKING WITH 5s AND 10s

The **5s and the 10s facts** are closely related. So even if you forget a 5s fact, it is easy to work out using a 10s fact.

The pattern in the **10s counting sequence** is really easy to remember. The numbers **always end with a zero**.

10 20 30 40 50 60 70 80 90 100 110 120 ...

Look at these matching 10s and 5s facts carefully.

$10 \times 1 = 10$	$5 \times 2 = 10$
$10 \times 2 = 20$	$5 \times 4 = 20$
$10 \times 6 = 60$	$5 \times 12 = 60$

Did you notice that there are **twice** as many 5s in each 5s fact as there are 10s in each matching 10s fact?

For example, there are **two 10s** in $10 \times 2 = 20$ and there are **four 5s** in $5 \times 4 = 20$.

There are **six 10s** in $10 \times 6 = 60$ and there are **twelve 5s** in $5 \times 12 = 60$.

We practise

Write the matching 5s fact for each 10s fact.

10×4	$5 \times 8 = 40$
10×3	$5 \times 6 = 30$

Write the matching 10s fact for each 5s fact.

5×4	$10 \times 2 = 20$
5×8	$10 \times 4 = 40$

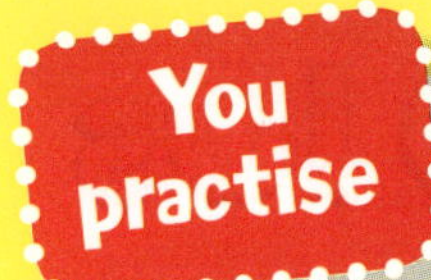

Write the matching 5s fact and the answer.

10 × 5 ____ × ____ = ____

10 × 3 ____ × ____ = ____

10 × 6 ____ × ____ = ____

10 × 4 ____ × ____ = ____

10 × 10 ____ × ____ = ____

Remember, there are **twice as many 5s** as there are **10s**.

Write the matching 10s fact and the answer.

5 × 2 ____ × ____ = ____

5 × 6 ____ × ____ = ____

5 × 10 ____ × ____ = ____

5 × 0 ____ × ____ = ____

5 × 12 ____ × ____ = ____

BOB time!

WORKING WITH 0s AND 1s

The **0s and 1s** are the easiest multiplication facts of all and yet they are the facts that **trick people** the most.

WRONG 1 × 3 = 4

3 × 1 = 4

CORRECT 1 × 3 = 3

3 × 1 = 3

Some people try to work out **3 × 1** by **adding** the two numbers instead of **multiplying** them.

To help you with 1s facts, look at this diagram for **3 × 1**.

  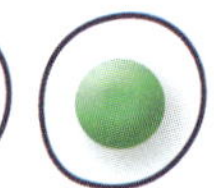

There are **3 groups** with **1 counter** in each group.

Now look at this diagram for **1 × 3**.

There is only **1 group** with **3 counters** in the group.

WRONG 0 × 7 = 7

7 × 0 = 7

CORRECT 0 × 7 = 0

7 × 0 = 0

When working out a 0s multiplication fact, such as **0 × 7**, a lot of people do not stop and think – they just say 7.

But if you have no groups then you have nothing, so the answer is 0, and if you have 7 groups with nothing in each group, then you have nothing at all – another big 0.

Tick the correct answers.
Write the correct answers next to the wrong answers.

✗ 6 × 1 = 7 6	✓ 1 × 4 = 4	✓ 5 × 1 = 5
✗ 0 × 3 = 3 0	✓ 0 × 9 = 0	✗ 6 × 0 = 6 0

You practise

Tick the correct answers.
Write the correct answer next to the wrong answers.

 1 $6 \times 1 = 6$

 2 $4 \times 1 = 5$

 3 $1 \times 5 = 5$

 4 $3 \times 1 = 4$

 5 $7 \times 1 = 7$

 6 $1 \times 8 = 8$

7 $2 \times 1 = 3$

 8 $10 \times 1 = 10$

9 $1 \times 9 = 10$

 10 $1 \times 20 = 21$

Remember to **multiply** not **add**. Don't be tricked!

You practise

Tick the correct answers.
Write the correct answer next to the wrong answers.

 11 $0 \times 7 = 7$

 12 $3 \times 0 = 0$

 13 $4 \times 0 = 4$

 14 $0 \times 8 = 8$

 15 $0 \times 9 = 0$

 16 $10 \times 0 = 10$

 17 $0 \times 13 = 13$

 18 $15 \times 0 = 0$

19 $25 \times 0 = 25$

 20 $0 \times 100 = 100$

Remember that zero means nothing!

BOB time!

WORKING WITH 2s AND 4s

2 × 4 = 8 double 4 is 8

2 × 5 = 10 double 5 is 10

Look at these **2s and 4s facts**. Do you see a **pattern**?

2 × 0 = 0	4 × 0 = 0
2 × 1 = 2	
2 × 2 = 4	4 × 1 = 4
2 × 3 = 6	
2 × 4 = 8	4 × 2 = 8
2 × 5 = 10	
2 × 6 = 12	4 × 3 = 12

Did you notice that **every second** fact in the 2s facts is also in the 4s facts?

To work out any 4s fact you can just **double the matching 2s fact**.
This is called a **double double**. The diagram below shows how it works.

4 × 3

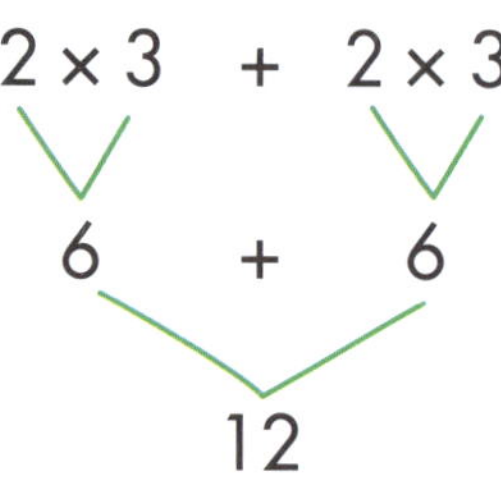

This is the same as **2 × 6 = 12**.

Learning the **2s facts** is easy because multiplying by 2 is the same as **doubling**.

We practise

Show the double double for 4 × 6.

2 × 6 + 2 × 6

12 + 12

24

This is the same as 2 × 12 = 24

Which 2s fact helps to work out 4 × 4?

2 × 4 = 8, then double to get 16

4 × 4 = 16

Show the double double for these multiplication facts.

1 4 × 7

2 × + 2 ×

+

3 4 × 9

2 × + 2 ×

+

2 4 × 8

2 × + 2 ×

+

4 4 × 5

2 × + 2 ×

+

You practise

Which 2s facts help to work out these 4s facts?

5 4 × 2 2 × _____ = _____ double to get _____

6 4 × 6 2 × _____ = _____ double to get _____

7 4 × 5 2 × _____ = _____ double to get _____

8 4 × 3 2 × _____ = _____ double to get _____

9 4 × 7 2 × _____ = _____ double to get _____

10 4 × 4 2 × _____ = _____ double to get _____

BOB time!

MASTERING THE 3s FACTS

You already know some of the **3s facts**. Look here to see why.

3 × 1 = 3 is the **turnaround** for 1 × 3 = 3

3 × 2 = 6 is the **turnaround** for 2 × 3 = 6

3 × 4 = 12 is the **turnaround** for 4 × 3 = 12

3 × 5 = 15 is the **turnaround** for 5 × 3 = 15

3 × 10 = 30 is the **turnaround** for 10 × 3 = 30

So that leaves only five 3s facts to learn.
These are also easy to learn.

A **square number** is the product you get when you multiply a number by itself.

3 × 3 = 9 9 is a **square number**, so just draw a square:

3 × 6 = 18 think 3 × 3 = 9, then **double** 9 (9 × 2 = 18)

3 × 7 = 21 think 2 × 7 =14 (**double** 7), then **add** 7 (14 + 7 = 21)

3 × 8 = 24 think 2 × 8 = 16 (**double** 8), then **add** 8 (16 + 8 = 24)

3 × 9 = 27 think 3 × 8 = 24, then **add** 3 (24 + 3 = 27)

We practise

You know 3 × 8 = 24.
To find 3 × 9 what do you need to do to 24?

24 + 3 = 27

You know 3 × 3 = 9.
To find 3 × 6 what do you need to do to 9?

9 × 2 = 18

You practise

Which known fact will help you to work out each 3s fact?

 3 × 1 ____ × ____ = ____

 3 × 5 ____ × ____ = ____

 3 × 10 ____ × ____ = ____

 3 × 2 ____ × ____ = ____

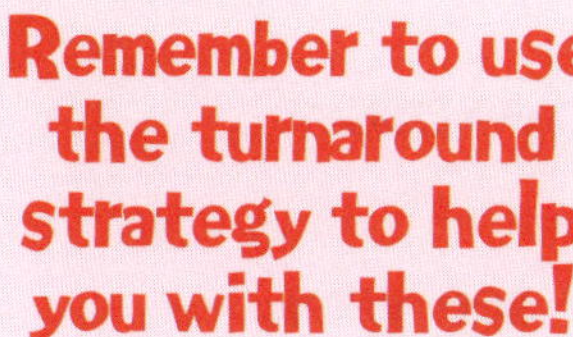

You practise

Show how you can use the known fact to help you work out each 3s fact.

 Use 3 × 3 = 9 to work out 3 × 6

9 ___ ____ = ____

 Use 3 × 8 = 24 to work out 3 × 9

24 ___ ____ = ____

 Use 2 × 8 = 16 to work out 3 × 8

16 ___ ____ = ____

 Which strategy would you use to work out 3 × 3?

BOB time!

LET'S GET SPEEDY

First say your 2s facts, and then 3s, 4s and 5s. Circle any that you were slow to remember – practise these ones to play **beat the calculator**.

Now it is time to see if you can get really speedy with the **2s, 3s, 4s and 5s facts**. The grid below will help you to get started.

×	0	1	2	3	4	5	6	7	8	9	10
2	0	2	4	6	8	10	12	14	16	18	20
3	0	3	6	9	12	15	18	21	24	27	30
4	0	4	8	12	16	20	24	28	32	36	40
5	0	5	10	15	20	25	30	35	40	45	50

Play **beat the calculator** with a partner. Your partner asks you multiplication facts from the table. Then you try to answer them before your partner has time to get the answer on the calculator.

Whoever is fastest scores 1 point and the first person to score 10 points is the winner.

You can also use this grid to answer questions such as:

Question **If the product is 15, what is the multiplication fact?**

To get the answer you put your finger on the product **15**, then follow the row and the column to find **5** and **3**.

Answer **3 × 5 or 5 × 3**

The answer to a multiplication question is the **product**.

We practise

Write a multiplication fact for each product.

12 = 3 × 4

15 = 3 × 5

Complete these multiplication facts as fast as you can.

3 × 3 = 9

4 × 4 = 16

5 × 5 = 25

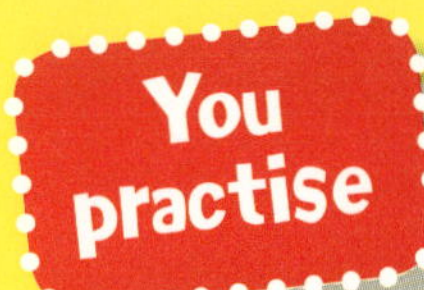

Complete these multiplication facts as fast as you can.

1. 4 × ___ = 8

2. ___ × 3 = 9

3. 6 × ___ = 18

4. 3 × 7 = _____

5. ___ × 7 = 28

6. 5 × ___ = 30

7. 4 × ___ = 36

8. ___ × 9 = 18

9. ___ × 6 = 18

10. 4 × 9 = _____

Use the grid if you need to.

You practise

Write a multiplication fact for each product.

11. 35 ___ × ___

12. 21 ___ × ___

13. 27 ___ × ___

14. 32 ___ × ___

15. 28 ___ × ___

BOB time!

PROBLEM SOLVING

Clare put the paintbrushes into 4 pots, with 8 brushes in each pot. Then she found 5 more paintbrushes. How many brushes are there altogether?

Notice that the important information is highlighted in blue and what has to be found out is highlighted in pink.

Drawing a diagram is one way of solving this problem.

You can also write a **number sentence** to solve this problem.

$4 \times 8 = 32$ $32 + 5 = 37$

There are 37 paintbrushes altogether.

We practise

Highlight the important information and what has to be found out in this problem.

Jake's team scored 3 wins worth 5 points each. They also scored 4 draws worth 3 points each. They need 30 points to go though to the next round. Will they make it through if they draw the next game?

Write multiplication facts to solve the problem.

$3 \times 5 = 15$ $4 \times 3 = 12$ $15 + 12 = 27$ $30 - 27 = 3$

Yes, they will make it through.

You practise

Highlight the important information and solve the problems using multiplication facts.

1. There are 3 pizzas and each one is cut into eighths. How many slices are there altogether? _____ slices

2. Jake keeps his collector cars in boxes. He has 4 boxes with 8 cars in each and 3 boxes with 6 cars in each. How many cars does he have? _____ cars

3. In the beanbag toss game Clare threw three 4s, six 5s and two 9s. Jake threw three 7s, three 8s and five 3s. Who won the game? ______________________________

4. Jake has four 5c coins and six 10c coins. Clare has three 5c coins and seven 10c coins. Who has most money and by how much? ____________ by ______

5. There are 4 boxes with 8 chocolates in each and 3 boxes with 6 chocolates in each. How many chocolates are there altogether? _____ chocolates

6. Clare needs 48 cards. Each box of cards holds 8 cards. How many boxes should she buy? _____ boxes

7. The fish tank holds 3 crabs (10 legs each), 4 octopi (8 legs each) and 5 starfish (5 legs each). How many legs are in the tank altogether? _____ legs

8. There are 3 cards with 4 large buttons on each, 4 cards with 6 medium buttons on each and 4 cards with 9 small buttons on each. How many buttons are there altogether? _____ buttons

9. Colour-change felt pens come in packets of 12. In each packet there are 3 colour-change pens, 2 eraser pens and the rest are plain colours. The teacher bought 4 packets. How many plain colours and how many colour-change pens does she have? _____ plain and _____ colour-change

10. If the product is 24, what are four possible multiplication facts?
____ × ____ ____ × ____ ____ × ____ ____ × ____

BOB time!

TURNAROUNDS

You may know more multiplication facts than you think you do because you also know their **turnarounds**.

For example, if you know **2 × 6 = 12**, then you also know its **turnaround 6 × 2 = 12**.

Just to prove that turnarounds always work, look at these diagrams.

3 rows of 4

3 × 4 = 12

turnaround to see 4 rows of 3

4 × 3 = 12

Both have **12** as their **product**.

Turnarounds have the **same numbers**, but in a **different order**.

Good news! There are **100 multiplication facts** to learn and you already know 60 and lots of turnarounds.

We practise

Complete each multiplication fact and write the turnaround.

2 × 6 = 12   6 × 2 = 12

4 × 7 = 28   7 × 4 = 28

5 × 8 = 40   8 × 5 = 40

Write the turnarounds that will help you with these multiplication facts.

7 × 3   3 × 7 = 21

8 × 2   2 × 8 = 16

6 × 4   4 × 6 = 24

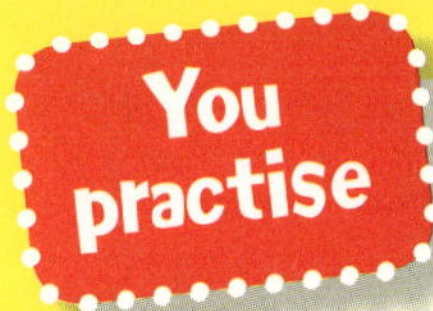

Use this multiplication chart to see how many facts you already know.

Shade all the **0s and 1s facts** across the row and down the column.

×	0	1	2	3	4	5	6	7	8	9	10
2	0	2	4	6	8	10	12	14	16	18	20
3	0	3	6	9	12	15	18	21	24	27	30
4	0	4	8	12	16	20	24	28	32	36	40
5	0	5	10	15	20	25	30	35	40	45	50
6	0	6	12	18	24	30	36	42	48	54	60
7	0	7	14	21	28	35	42	49	56	63	70
8	0	8	16	24	32	40	48	56	64	72	80
9	0	9	18	27	36	45	54	63	72	81	90
10	0	10	20	30	40	50	60	70	80	90	100

Then shade the **2s, 3s, 4s, 5s and 10s facts** in the same way.

How many facts are left to learn? ______

BOB time!

MASTERING THE 6s FACTS

There are seven **6s facts** that you already know from **turnarounds**:

$6 \times 0 = 0$

$6 \times 1 = 6$

$6 \times 2 = 12$

$6 \times 3 = 18$

$6 \times 4 = 24$

$6 \times 5 = 30$

$6 \times 10 = 60$

You can use **close-by 5s facts** to learn the others.

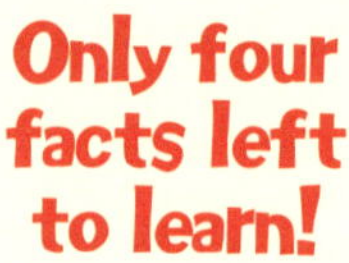

Look at this tally that shows **6 × 5**, which you know is **30**.

卌 卌 卌 卌 卌 卌

Now look at this tally showing **6 × 6**.

卌| 卌| 卌| 卌| 卌| 卌|

There are **6 extra tallies** in this diagram, so to find **6 × 6** you can follow these steps:

Step 1 $6 \times 5 = 30$

Step 2 $6 \times 1 = 6$

Step 3 $30 + 6 = 36$

Draw the tally for 6 × 7 and show the steps for working out the answer using a close-by 5s fact.

卌|| 卌|| 卌|| 卌|| 卌|| 卌||

Step 1 $6 \times 5 = 30$

Step 2 $6 \times 2 = 12$

Step 3 $30 + 12 = 42$

We practise

What is the multiplication fact for this tally? Use the close-by 5s fact to work out the answer.

卌||| 卌||| 卌||| 卌||| 卌||| 卌|||

6×8

Step 1 $6 \times 5 = 30$

Step 2 $6 \times 3 = 18$

Step 3 $30 + 18 = 48$

You practise Draw the tally for each multiplication fact and show the steps for working out the answer using a close-by 5s fact.

6 × 7

____ × ____ = ____

____ × ____ = ____

____ + ____ = ____

Remember to use a **close-by 5s fact** to help you.

6 × 8

____ × ____ = ____

____ × ____ = ____

____ + ____ = ____

6 × 9

____ × ____ = ____

____ × ____ = ____

____ + ____ = ____

You practise What is the multiplication fact for each tally?

卌 | 卌 | 卌 | 卌 |

____ × ____ = ____

卌 || 卌 || 卌 || 卌 || 卌 || 卌 ||

____ × ____ = ____

卌 |||| 卌 |||| 卌 |||| 卌 |||| 卌 |||| 卌 ||||

____ × ____ = ____

BOB time!

MASTERING THE 9s FACTS

Mastering the 9s facts is easy if you use the close-by 10s facts.

The tally below shows **2 groups of 9** (or 2 × 9).

卌 |||| 卌 ||||

If you add two more marks to the tally (shown in red) it shows **2 × 10**.

卌 卌   卌 卌

So to work out **2 × 9** using a **close-by 10s fact**, all you have to do is:

2 × 10 = 20

20 − 2 = 18

Tallies make it easy to see how to work from the 10s down to the 9s.

Here's another example. This tally shows 4 × 9.

卌 |||| 卌 |||| 卌 |||| 卌 ||||

If you add four more marks to the tally (shown in red) it shows **4 × 10**.

卌 卌   卌 卌   卌 卌   卌 卌

So to work out **4 × 9** using a **close-by 10s fact**, all you have to do is:

4 × 10 = 40

40 − 4 = 36

Use a close-by 10s fact to find 9 × 3. Draw the tally and then complete the facts.

卌 卌   卌 卌   卌 卌

3 × 10 = 30

30 − 3 = 27

9 × 3 = 27

We practise

Work out 9 × 7 using a close-by 10s fact.

7 × 10 = 70

70 − 7 = 63

9 × 7 = 63

You practise Use a close-by 10s fact to complete these 9s facts.

9 × 6

____ × 10 = ____

____ – ____ = ____

9 × 6 = ____

9 × 7

____ × 10 = ____

____ – ____ = ____

9 × 7 = ____

3

9 × 8

____ × 10 = ____

____ – ____ = ____

9 × 8 = ____

9 × 9

____ × 10 = ____

____ – ____ = ____

9 × 9 = ____

Answer these 9s facts as fast as you can.
Draw a star next to the ones you answered the fastest.

9 × 3 = ____

9 × 6 = ____

9 × 2 = ____

9 × 4 = ____

9 × 5 = ____

9 × 7 = ____

11

9 × 8 = ____

12

9 × 9 = ____

Use the **close-by 10s facts** to help you with the ones you don't know.

MASTERING THE 8s FACTS

Here is a list of the 8s facts that you already know from turnarounds, double doubles or close-by facts.

8 × 0 = 0	8 × 5 = 40
8 × 1 = 8	8 × 6 = 48
8 × 2 = 16	8 × 9 = 72
8 × 3 = 24	8 × 10 = 80
8 × 4 = 32	

The only **two left** to learn are:

8 × 7 = 56 **8 × 8 = 64**

Here are two ways to help you remember these two facts.

For **8 × 7**, think **5, 6, 7, 8,** which will remind you that **56 = 7 × 8**, which is the same as **8 × 7 = 56**.

For **8 × 8**, look at these counters arranged in a **square**.

To remember **8 × 8 = 64**, think of a **square**.

Then move the bottom two rows alongside the top 6 rows, making **6 rows of 10** with **4** left over.

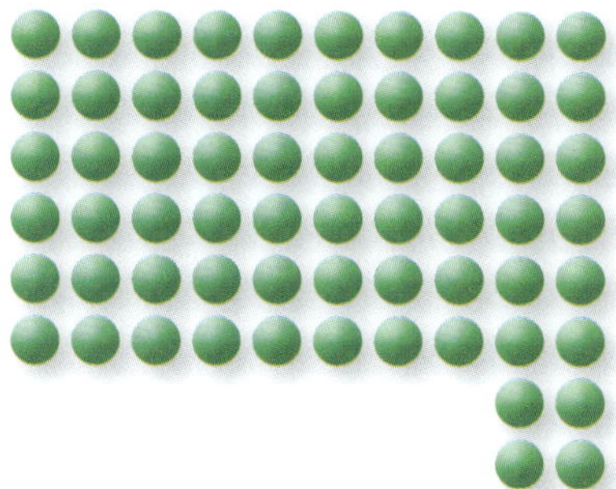

When you have learnt these two facts, you will know all of your 8s facts.

Write the turnaround and product for 8 × 4.

4 × 8 = 32

8 × 4 = 32

Write the 8s fact and the turnaround for this product.

8 × 6 = 48

6 × 8 = 48

We practise

Back to Basics

MULTIPLICATION TABLES

YEARS 4 and 5

Back to Basics
MULTIPLICATION TABLES
YEARS 4 and 5
Back to Basics
MULTIPLICATION TABLES
YEARS 4 and 5
Back to Basics
MULTIPLICATION TABLES
YEARS 4 and 5
Back to Basics
MULTIPLICATION TABLES
YEARS 4 and 5
Back to Basics
MULTIPLICATION TABLES
YEARS 4 and 5
Back to Basics
MULTIPLICATION TABLES
YEARS 4 and 5
Back to Basics
MULTIPLICATION TABLES
YEARS 4 and 5
Back to Basics
MULTIPLICATION TABLES
YEARS 4 and 5
Back to Basics
MULTIPLICATION TABLES
YEARS 4 and 5
Back to Basics
MULTIPLICATION TABLES
YEARS 4 and 5
Back to Basics
MULTIPLICATION TABLES
YEARS 4 and 5
Back to Basics
MULTIPLICATION TABLES
YEARS 4 and 5
Back to Basics
MULTIPLICATION TABLES
YEARS 4 and 5
Back to Basics
MULTIPLICATION TABLES
YEARS 4 and 5
Back to Basics
MULTIPLICATION TABLES
YEARS 4 and 5

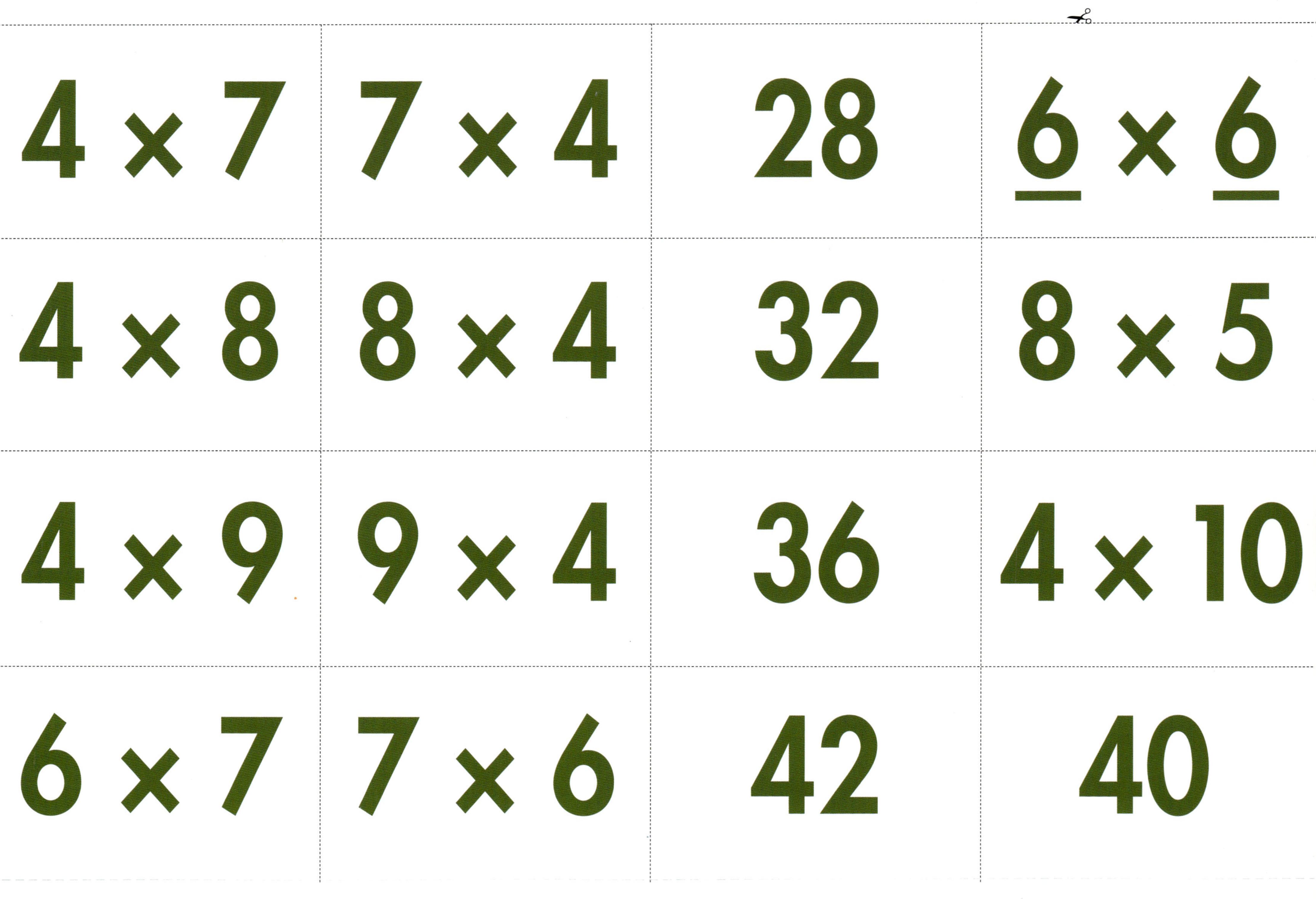
4 × 7
7 × 4
28
6 × 6
4 × 8
8 × 4
32
8 × 5
4 × 9
9 × 4
36
4 × 10
6 × 7
7 × 6
42
40

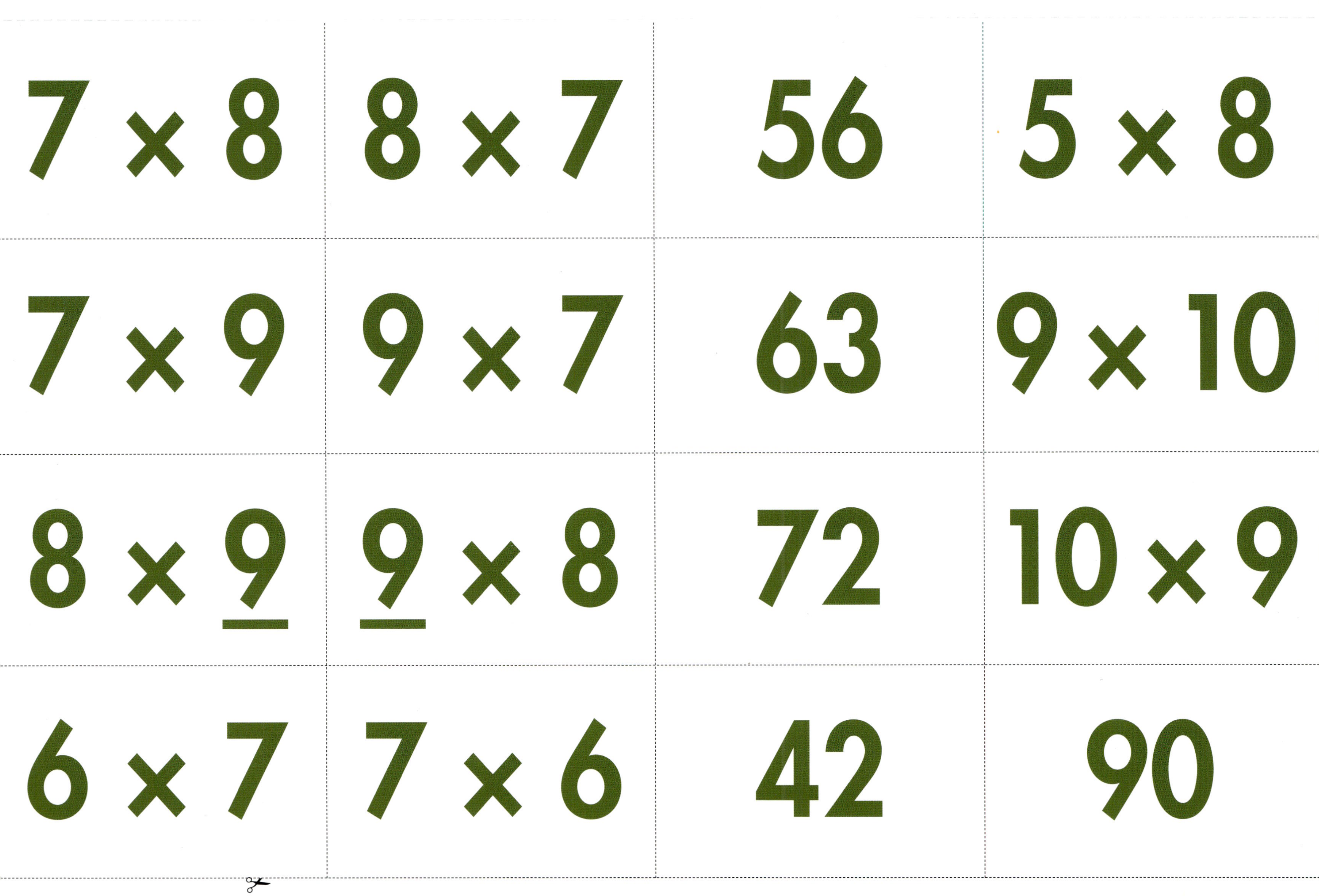

7 × 8
8 × 7
56
5 × 8
7 × 9
9 × 7
63
9 × 10
8 × 9
9 × 8
72
10 × 9
6 × 7
7 × 6
42
90

MULTIPLICATION TABLES

YEARS 4 and 5

Back to Basics

MULTIPLICATION TABLES

YEARS 4 and 5

MULTIPLICATION TABLES

YEARS 4 and 5

MULTIPLICATION TABLES

YEARS 4 and 5

Back to Basics

MULTIPLICATION TABLES

YEARS 4 and 5

Back to Basics

MULTIPLICATION TABLES

YEARS 4 and 5

Back to Basics

MULTIPLICATION TABLES

YEARS 4 and 5

MULTIPLICATION TABLES

YEARS 4 and 5

MULTIPLICATION TABLES

YEARS 4 and 5

Back to Basics

MULTIPLICATION TABLES

YEARS 4 and 5

MULTIPLICATION TABLES

YEARS 4 and 5

MULTIPLICATION TABLES

YEARS 4 and 5

MULTIPLICATION TABLES

YEARS 4 and 5

Back to Basics

MULTIPLICATION TABLES

YEARS 4 and 5

Back to Basics

MULTIPLICATION TABLES

YEARS 4 and 5

MULTIPLICATION TABLES

YEARS 4 and 5

You practise

Write the turnaround and product for each 8s fact.

8 × 2 ___ × ___ = ____ 8 × 2 = ____

8 × 5 ___ × ___ = ____ 8 × 5 = ____

8 × 9 ___ × ___ = ____ 8 × 9 = ____

8 × 3 ___ × ___ = ____ 8 × 3 = ____

8 × 4 ___ × ___ = ____ 8 × 4 = ____

Write the 8s fact and its turnaround for each product.

8 × ___ = 48 ___ × ___ = 48

8 × ___ = 64 ___ × ___ = 64

8 × ___ = 80 ___ × ___ = 80

8 × ___ = 32 ___ × ___ = 32

8 × ___ = 56 ___ × ___ = 56

MASTERING THE 7s FACTS

Here are the **7s facts** that you already know from their **turnarounds**.

7 × 0 = 0	0 × 7 = 0
7 × 1 = 7	1 × 7 = 7
7 × 2 = 14	2 × 7 = 14
7 × 3 = 21	3 × 7 = 21
7 × 4 = 28	4 × 7 = 28
7 × 5 = 35	5 × 7 = 35
7 × 6 = 42	6 × 7 = 42
7 × 7 = 49	
7 × 8 = 56	8 × 7 = 56
7 × 9 = 63	9 × 7 = 63
7 × 10 = 70	10 × 7 = 70

Guess what! You already know all but one of your **7s facts**!

This is the one that you may not know yet. It's a **square number** and I love square numbers!

So all that's left is 7 × 7. Look at these counters arranged in a **7 × 7 square**.

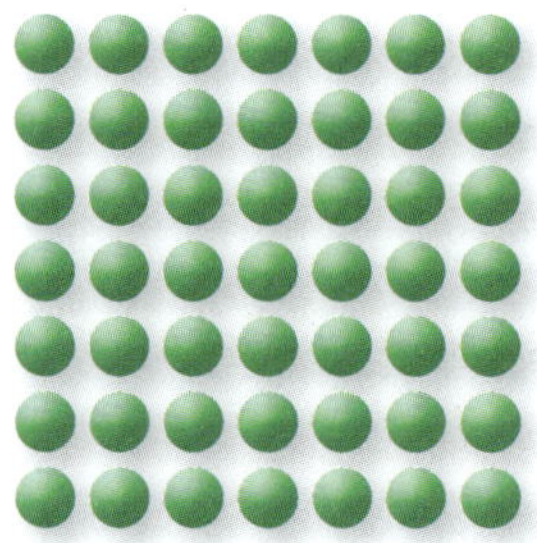

To help you remember **7 × 7 = 49**, think of a **square**.

Then move the bottom 3 rows alongside the top 4 rows, making **4 rows of 10** with **9** left over.

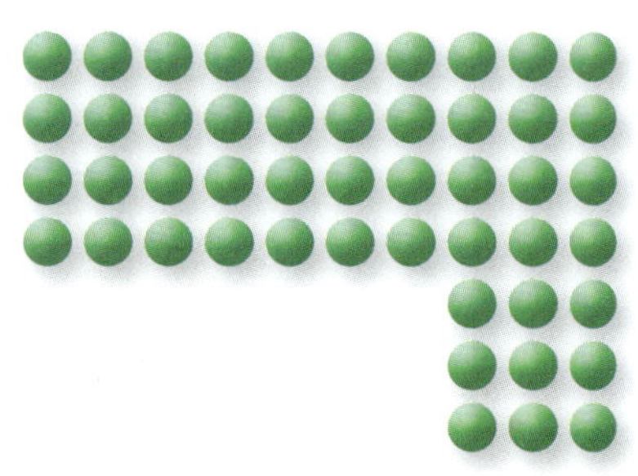

Write the 7s fact and the turnaround for this product.

63 = 7 × 9

63 = 9 × 7

Write the turnaround and product for 7 × 6.

6 × 7 = 42

7 × 6 = 42

You practise Complete these 7s facts. Circle any facts that you don't know and practise them later.

 1. $7 \times 7 =$ ____

 2. $7 \times 0 =$ ____

 3. $7 \times 4 =$ ____

 4. $7 \times 5 =$ ____

 5. $7 \times 6 =$ ____

 6. $7 \times 9 =$ ____

 7. $7 \times 1 =$ ____

8. $7 \times 10 =$ ____

9. $7 \times 8 =$ ____

10. $7 \times 3 =$ ____

11. $7 \times 2 =$ ____

Make sure you don't look at the 7s facts on the opposite page!

You practise What is the 7s fact for each product?

 12. $49 =$ ____ $\times$ ____

 13. $28 =$ ____ $\times$ ____

 14. $56 =$ ____ $\times$ ____

 15. $63 =$ ____ $\times$ ____

 16. $21 =$ ____ $\times$ ____

 17. $42 =$ ____ $\times$ ____

18. $14 =$ ____ $\times$ ____

19. $35 =$ ____ $\times$ ____

20. $7 =$ ____ $\times$ ____

UNIT 13

MORE LET'S GET SPEEDY

Now it's time to make sure that you really know your **6s, 7s, 8s** and **9s facts**.
Practice makes perfect!

Say the 6s facts and circle any facts in the grid below that you didn't know instantly.

×	0	1	2	3	4	5	6	7	8	9	10
6	0	6	12	18	24	30	36	42	48	54	60
7	0	7	14	21	28	35	42	49	56	63	70
8	0	8	16	24	32	40	48	56	64	72	80
9	0	9	18	27	36	45	54	63	72	81	90

Do the same with the **7s**, **8s** and **9s facts**.

Look back through this book and find the strategy that will help you to remember each circled fact.

Remember to think about **turnarounds** too.

We practise

Complete these multiplication facts as fast as you can.

8 × 9 = 72

6 × 8 = 48

6 × 7 = 42

Write a multiplication fact to match each product as fast as you can.

36 = 9 × 4

56 = 7 × 8

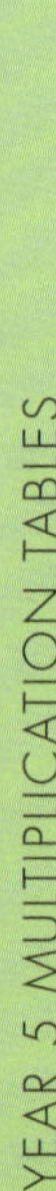

You practise

Complete these multiplication facts as fast as you can.

_____ × 8 = 48

7 × _____ = 56

9 × 9 = _____

8 × _____ = 48

_____ × 9 = 36

Try **saying the answers** while **someone times you**. Circle any that you need to work on before trying the speed test again.

You practise

Write a multiplication fact to match each product as fast as you can.

49 = _____ × _____

72 = _____ × _____

63 = _____ × _____

54 = _____ × _____

64 = _____ × _____

Remember to time yourself.

BOB time!

SPEEDING ALONG

It's time to check **which facts** you need to **practise**.

Recite all the facts. Shade the ones that you are really speedy and confident with.

×	0	1	2	3	4	5	6	7	8	9	10
3	0	3	6	9	12	15	18	21	24	27	30
4	0	4	8	12	16	20	24	28	32	36	40
5	0	5	10	15	20	25	30	35	40	45	50
6	0	6	12	18	24	30	36	42	48	54	60
7	0	7	14	21	28	35	42	49	56	63	70
8	0	8	16	24	32	40	48	56	64	72	80
9	0	9	18	27	36	45	54	63	72	81	90

Look back through this book and **find a strategy** that will help you with each one that you did not shade.

When you feel confident, play beat the calculator with a partner. Your partner calls out the facts from the grid and then you try to answer before your partner has time to get the answer on the calculator.

We practise

Complete these facts as fast as you can. Use the grid above to check your answers.

$3 \times 7 = 21$ $\quad$ $4 \times 8 = 32$

$6 \times 9 = 54$ $\quad$ $3 \times 8 = 24$

$4 \times 9 = 36$ $\quad$ $6 \times 8 = 48$

You practise

Try this speed test. Ask someone to time you while you complete these multiplication facts.

1. $8 \times 8 =$ _____

2. $7 \times 6 =$ _____

3. $9 \times 6 =$ _____

4. $9 \times 8 =$ _____

5. $8 \times 7 =$ _____

6. $6 \times 8 =$ _____

7. $7 \times 9 =$ _____

8. $8 \times 6 =$ _____

9. $7 \times 8 =$ _____

10. $7 \times 7 =$ _____

11. $8 \times 9 =$ _____

12. $6 \times 9 =$ _____

What is your personal best? _____ seconds

Circle the facts that you need to practise and then write each complete fact in the space below.

Say these facts to yourself a few times and then do the speed test again.

What is your new personal best?

_____ seconds

BOB time!

MULTIPLICATION and DIVISION

You can use multiplication facts to help you with division.

For example, to divide 18 marbles into 6 equal-sized groups (**18 ÷ 6**), you could use this diagram.

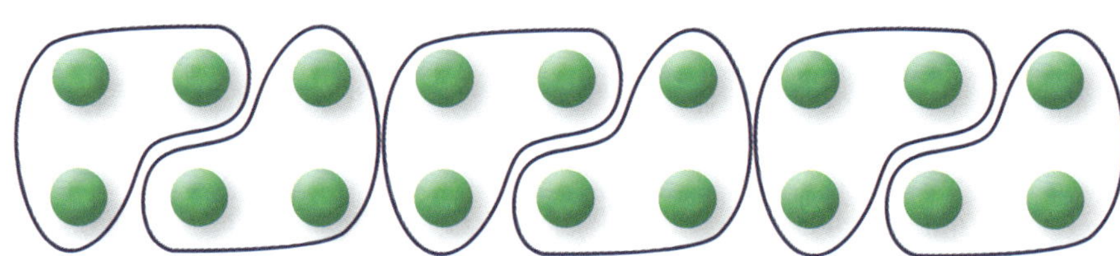

Did you notice that there are **6 groups** each with **3 marbles**? This is the same as **6 × 3 = 18**.

Knowing multiplication facts makes division easy!

For 42 ÷ 6 you can ask:

6 times what equals 42?

And you should know that **6 × 7 = 42**, so **42 ÷ 6 = 7**.

Related multiplication facts will help with all division questions. So every time you need to divide, say to yourself:

Which multiplication fact helps with this division fact?

We practise

Which multiplication fact helps with 45 ÷ 5?

5 × 9 = 45

45 ÷ 5 = 9

Complete these related division and multiplication facts.

36 ÷ 4 = 9

4 × 9 = 36

You practise

Which multiplication fact helps with each division fact?

 1 $36 \div 6 = 6$ ___ × ___ = ___

 2 $56 \div 7 = 8$ ___ × ___ = ___

 3 $49 \div 7 = 7$ ___ × ___ = ___

 4 $28 \div 7 = 4$ ___ × ___ = ___

 5 $63 \div 9 = 7$ ___ × ___ = ___

Look back at the **facts grid** if you need to.

You practise

Complete these related division and multiplication facts.

 6 $36 \div 6 =$ ___ ___ × ___ = ___

 7 $54 \div 9 =$ ___ ___ × ___ = ___

 8 $54 \div 6 =$ ___ ___ × ___ = ___

 9 $64 \div 8 =$ ___ ___ × ___ = ___

 10 $36 \div 4 =$ ___ ___ × ___ = ___

BOB time!

MULTIPLES and FACTORS

You already know that when you multiply two numbers the answer is called the product.

A **multiple** is similar to a **product**. For example:

$4 \times 2 = 8$

8 is the **product** and also a **multiple** of 4.

In fact, any number in the 4s facts is a multiple of 4. For example:

$4 \times 2 = 8$

$4 \times 3 = 12$

$4 \times 4 = 16$

The numbers **8**, **12**, **16** and so on are all **multiples of 4**.

Now it's time to learn about **multiples** and **factors**.

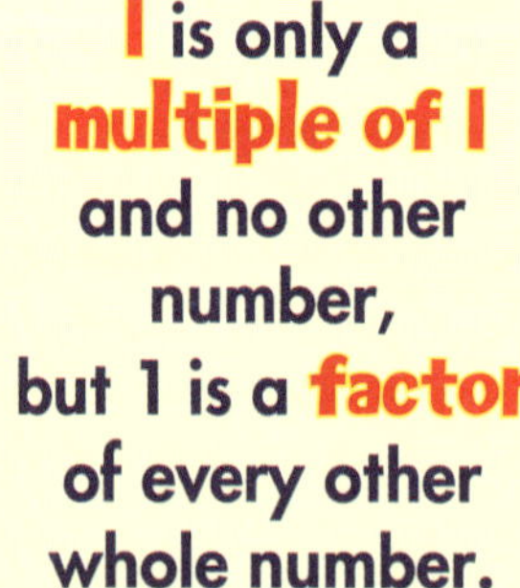

1 is only a multiple of 1 and no other number, but 1 is a factor of every other whole number.

A factor is the number that you multiply with another number to get the product.

For example, **6** has four factors:

$\mathbf{1} \times \mathbf{6} = 6$

$\mathbf{2} \times \mathbf{3} = 6$

$\mathbf{3} \times \mathbf{2} = 6$

$\mathbf{6} \times \mathbf{1} = 6$

The numbers **1**, **2**, **3** and **6** are all **factors of 6**.

The numbers **2** and **3** are **proper factors** of **6**, whereas **1** and **6** are just factors of 6.

1 is a factor of every whole number and every number is a factor of itself.

We practise

What are three multiples of each of these numbers?

2	6	10	12
3	9	12	21
7	21	28	42

What are two factors for each of these numbers?

4	1	2
27	3	9
15	3	5

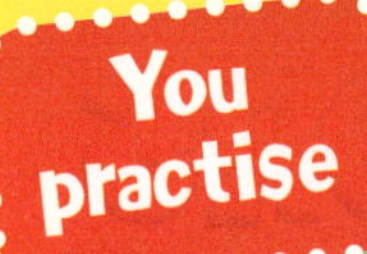

What are three multiples of each of these numbers?

 4 ____ ____ ____

 6 ____ ____ ____

 7 ____ ____ ____

 8 ____ ____ ____

 9 ____ ____ ____

If you are stuck, look back at the **multiplication grid** opposite.

You practise

What are two factors of each of these numbers?

 12 ____ ____

 24 ____ ____

 35 ____ ____

 42 ____ ____

 54 ____ ____

See if you can find **factors** that are **larger than 1**.

BOB time!

UNIT 17

MORE MULTIPLICATION and DIVISION

You are on your way to mastering multiplication and division.

You have already started learning about related **multiplication** and **division** facts and about **multiples** and **factors**.

Here are some pairs of multiplication and division facts:

3 × 7 = 21 21 ÷ 7 = 3

7 × 3 = 21 21 ÷ 3 = 7

These facts are like a family. Once you know one multiplication fact, you know its **turnaround** and the **related division facts**.

These are called a fact family because they are all related!

Some people think that division is harder than multiplication, but it isn't.

Fill in the missing operators (× or ÷) and missing numbers as you wind your way to find the missing middle number.

2	×	4	=	8
=	4	×	5	÷
3	=	2	=	4
÷	10	÷	20	=
12	=	6	×	2

Fill in the missing operators (× or ÷) and missing numbers as you wind your way to find the missing middle number.

24	÷		=	4
=	18		6	×
3	=		=	
	2	×		=
6	=	2		12

72	÷		=	9
=	30	÷		
5	=		=	2
	7		5	=
	=	3	÷	18

1		6	=	
=	32		4	×
	=		=	2
×	8	÷		=
	=		÷	

3	×		=	24
=	8			
	=		=	6
	8		32	=
40	=			4

3			=	24
=	8			
	=		=	6
	8		32	=
40	=			4

8			=	8
=	24	÷		
	=		=	
	8		6	=
12	=			4

MORE LET'S GET SPEEDY

Recite all the facts below as fast as you can. Shade the ones that you are really speedy and confident with.

It's time to check which **division facts** you need to **practise**.

3 ÷ 3 = 1	4 ÷ 4 = 1	5 ÷ 5 = 1	6 ÷ 6 = 1	7 ÷ 7 = 1	8 ÷ 8 = 1	9 ÷ 9 = 1
6 ÷ 3 = 2	8 ÷ 4 = 2	10 ÷ 5 = 2	12 ÷ 6 = 2	14 ÷ 7 = 2	16 ÷ 8 = 2	18 ÷ 9 = 2
9 ÷ 3 = 3	12 ÷ 4 = 3	15 ÷ 5 = 3	18 ÷ 6 = 3	21 ÷ 7 = 3	24 ÷ 8 = 3	27 ÷ 9 = 3
12 ÷ 3 = 4	16 ÷ 4 = 4	20 ÷ 5 = 4	24 ÷ 6 = 4	28 ÷ 7 = 4	32 ÷ 8 = 4	36 ÷ 9 = 4
15 ÷ 3 = 5	20 ÷ 4 = 5	25 ÷ 5 = 5	30 ÷ 6 = 5	35 ÷ 7 = 5	40 ÷ 8 = 5	45 ÷ 9 = 5
18 ÷ 3 = 6	24 ÷ 4 = 6	30 ÷ 5 = 6	36 ÷ 6 = 6	42 ÷ 7 = 6	48 ÷ 8 = 6	54 ÷ 9 = 6
21 ÷ 3 = 7	28 ÷ 4 = 7	35 ÷ 5 = 7	42 ÷ 6 = 7	49 ÷ 7 = 7	56 ÷ 8 = 7	63 ÷ 9 = 7
24 ÷ 3 = 8	32 ÷ 4 = 8	40 ÷ 5 = 8	48 ÷ 6 = 8	56 ÷ 7 = 8	64 ÷ 8 = 8	72 ÷ 9 = 8
27 ÷ 3 = 9	36 ÷ 4 = 9	45 ÷ 5 = 9	54 ÷ 6 = 9	63 ÷ 7 = 9	72 ÷ 8 = 9	81 ÷ 9 = 9
30 ÷ 3 = 10	40 ÷ 4 = 10	50 ÷ 5 = 10	60 ÷ 6 = 10	70 ÷ 7 = 10	80 ÷ 8 = 10	90 ÷ 9 = 10

We practise

Complete these division facts.

36 ÷ 6 = 6　　49 ÷ 7 = 7

54 ÷ 9 = 6　　42 ÷ 6 = 7

56 ÷ 7 = 8　　36 ÷ 4 = 9

When you feel confident, play beat the calculator with a partner.

Your partner calls out the facts from the table and then you try to answer before you partner has time to get the answer on the calculator.

Remember to use **known multiplication facts** to help with the division facts that you don't know.

You practise

Ask someone to time you while you complete these division facts.

 1. 28 ÷ 4 = ____

 2. 36 ÷ 9 = ____

 3. 54 ÷ 9 = ____

4. 81 ÷ 9 = ____

 5. 48 ÷ 6 = ____

 6. 36 ÷ 6 = ____

7. 56 ÷ 7 = ____

 8. 27 ÷ 9 = ____

9. 63 ÷ 9 = ____

10. 49 ÷ 7 = ____

Use the grid opposite to **check your answers**.

What is your personal best? ____ seconds

You practise

Complete these division facts as fast as you can.

 11. 49 ÷ ____ = 7

 12. 72 ÷ ____ = 8

 13. ____ ÷ 7 = 9

 14. 54 ÷ 9 = ____

 15. 64 ÷ ____ = 8

MIXED BAG

Now it's time to mix things up a bit.

Here are some **multiplication** and **division** questions mixed with **multiple** and **factor** questions. You need to read them carefully and pay attention to the **operators** (× and ÷) to make sure that you are not tripped up by any of the questions.

$6 \times 2 = 12$

$9 \times 3 = 27$

$10 \div 2 = 5$

$8 \times 4 = 32$

Beware! Look carefully at the operators.

Did you notice that one of the facts is a **division** fact and all of the others are **multiplication** facts?

Sometimes a division question is slipped in among multiplication questions in a test to see if you are paying attention.

Now read this question carefully:

Circle one factor in this number sentence: 2 × 4 = 8

There are actually **two factors** in the number sentence, but the question asks you to circle **one** factor (not **two** or **both**), so the **answer** is either **2** or **4**.

We practise

Complete these facts.

$4 \times 3 = 12$ $8 \times 2 = 16$

$16 \div 2 = 8$ $9 \div 3 = 3$

$9 + 4 = 13$

Circle the factors of 24.

   9

7  2

You practise

Answer these questions.

Watch out, there be might be a trick question!

 1. $10 \div 2 =$ ____

 2. $6 \times 2 =$ ____

 3. $6 \times 7 =$ ____

 4. $12 \div 2 =$ ____

 5. $15 \div 5 =$ ____

 6. $9 \div 3 =$ ____

 7. 5 is one factor of 15. What is the other factor? ____

 8. What is the lowest multiple of 3, 4, 2 and 6? ____

 9. What are two factors of 24? ____ ____

 10. $36 \div 9 =$ ____

 11. $9 \times 3 =$ ____

 12. 4×6 and 3×8 both have 24 as their product. True or false? ________

 13. $9 \div 9 =$ ____

 14. List all the factors of 12. ____ ____ ____ ____ ____ ____

 15. What is the product of 9 and 7? ____

UNIT 20

MORE PROBLEM SOLVING

Clare made 6 bags with 6 treats in each bag. Jake had the same number of treats, but he made bags with 4 treats in each bag. How many bags of treats did Jake make?

Notice that the important information is highlighted in blue and what has to be found out is highlighted in pink.

To work out how many bags of treats Jake made, you could use these steps.

Step 1 How many treats altogether does Clare have?

$6 \times 6 = \mathbf{36}$

Step 2 How many bags of 4 treats can be made from 36 treats?

$36 \div 4 = \mathbf{9}$

Answer: Jake made 9 bags of treats.

Highlight the important information and what has to be found out in this problem. Then solve the problem and complete the answer sentence.

Clare has 48 lollies to share between herself, her brother and their 4 friends. How many lollies can each person have?

Step 1 How many people have to share the lollies? $1 + 1 + 4 = 6$

Step 2 How many treats are there altogether? $48 \div 6 = 8$

Each person gets 8 lollies each.

You practise

Highlight the important information and solve these problems using multiplication or division.

Remember to stop and think whether it is a multiplication or a division problem.

1 Clare bought 6 pairs of socks at $6 a pair.
How much change should she receive from $40? $____

2 Jake bought 3 pairs of socks at $8 a pair and 4 pairs at $5 a pair. How much change should he receive from $50? $____

3 Clare and Jake are going away for a week. They need to leave enough food for their spoilt dog with their neighbour. Every day the dog has 6 chocolate drops, 4 chews and 9 dog biscuits. How many of each item are needed for the week?
____ chocolate drops ____ chews ____ dog biscuits

4 Closest to 100 is a game that Clare and Jake play. They each throw a dice 20 times and record each throw. The person with the highest score is the winner. Yesterday Clare threw six 3s, four 5s, three 6s and seven 4s. Jake threw three 1s, five 5s, four 6s and eight 3s. Who was closest to 100 and by how much?
______________ by _____

5 There are two fish tanks at the pet shop. One tank has 6 squid (10 arms each) and the other has 8 octopuses (8 arms each). Which tank has the most arms?
____

6 Dad said, "You can have $8 a week for 6 weeks or you can have $3 every 3 days for 8 weeks." Which is the better deal? ______________

7 Clare has $24 for her 4-day holiday. She plans to spend the same amount of money each day. How much money can she spend each day? _______

8 This year there are 48 fairy cakes for the school fair. They must be shared into equal-sized packets (with more than two cakes per packet) and as many packets as possible. How can this be done? ______________

9 64 felt pens were spilt on the floor. "Please pick them up and put the same amount of pens into 8 tubs," the teacher said. How many pens should be put into each tub? ______________

10 The number I am thinking of has 3 factors.
It is a single digit number. 9 is one of its multiples.
What is the number? ______

BOB time!

TEST 1

5 × 9 = ____

5 × 7 = ____

5 × 6 = ____

10 × 6 = ____

10 × 1 = ____

10 × 7 = ____

1 × 7 = ____

0 × 6 = ____

5 × 0 = ____

What is the double double for this multiplication fact?

4 × 8

2 × ____ = ____

2 × ____ = ____

What is the double double for this multiplication fact?

4 × 7

2 × ____ = ____

2 × ____ = ____

Write the multiplication fact for this tally.

卌 卌 卌 卌
| | | |

____ × ____ = ____

Write the multiplication fact for this tally.

卌 卌 卌 卌 卌
|||| |||| |||| |||| ||||

____ × ____ = ____

9 × 6 = ____

9 × 9 = ____

9 × 5 = ____

7 × 9 = ____

8 × 9 = ____

TEST 2

What is the turnaround for this multiplication fact?

8 × 5 = ____

____ × ____ = ____

What is the turnaround for this multiplication fact?

8 × 9 = ____

____ × ____ = ____

7 × 7 = ____

7 × 1 = ____

7 × 4 = ____

6 × 6 = ____

6 × 9 = ____

6 × 7 = ____

48 = 6 × ____

56 = 7 × ____

81 = ____ × ____

Write the multiplication fact that helps with this division fact.

45 ÷ 9 = ____

9 × ____ = 45

Write the multiplication fact that helps with this division fact.

36 ÷ 4 = ____

4 × ____ = 36

Write the multiplication fact that helps with this division fact.

36 ÷ 6 = ____

6 × ____ = 36

What are the four proper factors for the number 12?

____ × ____ = 12

____ × ____ = 12

ANSWERS

Unit 1

1 45 ✓
2 20
3 55 ✓
4 35 ✓
5 10
6 5 ✓
7 60
8 15 ✓
9 50
10 25 ✓
11 10 ✓
12 15
13 35
14 60 ✓
15 50 ✓
16 25
17 30 ✓
18 40 ✓
19 5
20 20 ✓

Unit 2

1 5 × 10 = 50
2 5 × 6 = 30
3 5 × 12 = 60
4 5 × 8 = 40
5 5 × 20 = 100
6 10 × 1 = 10
7 10 × 3 = 30
8 10 × 5 = 50
9 10 × 0 = 0
10 10 × 6 = 60

Unit 3

1 6 × 1 = 6 ✓
2 4 × 1 = 5 4
3 1 × 5 = 5 ✓
4 3 × 1 = 4 3
5 7 × 1 = 7 ✓
6 1 × 8 = 8 ✓
7 2 × 1 = 3 2
8 10 × 1 = 10 ✓
9 1 × 9 = 10 9
10 1 × 20 = 21 20
11 0 × 7 = 7 0
12 3 × 0 = 0 ✓
13 4 × 0 = 4 0
14 0 × 8 = 8 0
15 0 × 9 = 0 ✓
16 10 × 0 = 10 0
17 0 × 13 = 13 0
18 15 × 0 = 0 ✓
19 25 × 0 = 25 0
20 0 × 100 = 100 0

Unit 4

1 2 × 7 + 2 × 7
14 + 14
28

2 2 × 8 + 2 × 8
16 + 16
32

3 2 × 9 + 2 × 9
18 + 18
36

4 2 × 5 + 2 × 5
10 + 10
20

5 2 × 2 = 4 double to get 8
6 2 × 6 = 12 double to get 24
7 2 × 5 = 10 double to get 20
8 2 × 3 = 6 double to get 12
9 2 × 7 = 14 double to get 28
10 2 × 4 = 8 double to get 16

Unit 5

1 1 × 3 = 3
2 5 × 3 = 15
3 10 × 3 = 30
4 2 × 3 = 6
5 9 × 2 = 18
6 24 + 3 = 27
7 16 + 8 = 24
8 Draw a square

Unit 6

1 4 × 2 = 8
2 3 × 3 = 9
3 6 × 3 = 18
4 3 × 7 = 21
5 4 × 7 = 28
6 5 × 6 = 30
7 4 × 9 = 36
8 2 × 9 = 18
9 3 × 6 = 18

ANSWERS

10 4 × 9 = 36
11 5 × 7 = 35
12 3 × 7 = 21
13 3 × 9 = 27
14 4 × 8 = 32
15 4 × 7 = 28

Unit 7

1 24 slices
2 50 cars
3 No one – it is a tie
4 Clare by 5c
5 50 chocolates
6 6 boxes
7 87
8 72 buttons
9 28 plain and 12 colour change
10 1 × 24 2 × 12 3 × 8 4 × 6
6 × 4 8 × 3 12 × 2 24 × 1

Unit 8

×	0	1	2	3	4	5	6	7	8	9	10
0	0	0	0	0	0	0	0	0	0	0	0
1	0	1	2	3	4	5	6	7	8	9	10
2	0	2	4	6	8	10	12	14	16	18	20
3	0	3	6	9	12	15	18	21	24	27	30
4	0	4	8	12	16	20	24	28	32	36	40
5	0	5	10	15	20	25	30	35	40	45	50
6	0	6	12	18	24	30	36	42	48	54	60
7	0	7	14	21	28	35	42	49	56	63	70
8	0	8	16	24	32	40	48	56	64	72	80
9	0	9	18	27	36	45	54	63	72	81	90
10	0	10	20	30	40	50	60	70	80	90	100

16

Unit 9

1 𝍸 𝍸 𝍸 𝍸 𝍸 𝍸
|| || || || || ||
6 × 5 = 30 6 × 2 = 12
30 + 12 = 42

2 𝍸 𝍸 𝍸 𝍸 𝍸 𝍸
||| ||| ||| ||| ||| |||
6 × 5 = 30 6 × 3 = 18
30 + 18 = 48

3 𝍸 𝍸 𝍸 𝍸 𝍸 𝍸
|||| |||| |||| |||| |||| ||||
6 × 5 = 30 6 × 4 = 24
30 + 24 = 54

4 6 × 4 = 24
5 6 × 7 = 42
6 6 × 9 = 72

Unit 10

1 6 × 10 = 60 60 – 6 = 54
9 × 6 = 54
2 7 × 10 = 70 70 – 7 = 63
9 × 7 = 63
3 8 × 10 = 80 80 – 8 = 72
9 × 8 = 72
4 9 × 10 = 90 90 – 9 = 81
9 × 9 = 81
5 9 × 3 = 27
6 9 × 6 = 54
7 9 × 2 = 18
8 9 × 4 = 36
9 9 × 5 = 45
10 9 × 7 = 63
11 9 × 8 = 72
12 9 × 9 = 81

Unit 11

1 2 × 8 =16 8 × 2 = 16
2 5 × 8 = 40 8 × 5 = 40
3 9 × 8 = 72 8 × 9 = 72
4 3 × 8 = 24 8 × 3 = 24
5 4 × 8 = 32 8 × 4 = 32
6 8 × 6 = 48 6 × 8 = 48
7 8 × 8 = 64 8 × 8 = 64
8 8 × 10 = 80 10 × 8 = 80
9 8 × 4 = 32 4 × 8 = 32
10 8 × 7 = 56 7 × 8 = 56

Unit 12

1 7 × 7 = 49
2 7 × 0 = 0
3 7 × 4 = 28
4 7 × 5 = 35
5 7 × 6 = 42
6 7 × 9 = 63
7 7 × 1 = 7
8 7 × 10 = 70
9 7 × 8 = 56
10 7 × 3 = 21
11 7 × 2 = 14
12 49 = 7 × 7
13 28 = 7 × 4
14 56 = 7 × 8
15 63 = 7 × 9
16 21 = 7 × 3

ANSWERS

17 42 = 7 × 6
18 14 = 7 × 2
19 35 = 7 × 5
20 7 = 7 × 1

Unit 13

1 6 × 8 = 48
2 7 × 8 = 56
3 9 × 9 = 81
4 8 × 6 = 48
5 4 × 9 = 36
6 49 = 7 × 7
7 72 = 8 × 9
8 63 = 9 × 7
9 54 = 6 × 9
10 64 = 8 × 8

Unit 14

1 8 × 8 = 64
2 7 × 6 = 42
3 9 × 6 = 54
4 9 × 8 = 72
5 8 × 7 = 56
6 6 × 8 = 48
7 7 × 9 = 63
8 8 × 6 = 48
9 7 × 8 = 56
10 7 × 7 = 49
11 8 × 9 = 72
12 6 × 9 = 54

Unit 15

1 6 × 6 = 36
2 7 × 8 = 56
3 7 × 7 = 49
4 7 × 4 = 28
5 9 × 7 = 63
6 36 ÷ 6 = 6 6 × 6 = 36
7 54 ÷ 9 = 6 9 × 6 = 54
8 54 ÷ 6 = 9 6 × 9 = 54
9 64 ÷ 8 = 8 8 × 8 = 64
10 36 ÷ 4 = 9 4 × 9 = 36

Unit 16

1 8 12 16
2 12 18 24
3 14 21 28
4 16 24 32
5 18 27 36
6 2 3
7 4 6
8 5 7
9 6 7
10 6 9

Unit 17

1

24	÷	6	=	4
=	18	÷	6	×
3	=	6	=	3
×	2	×	3	=
6	=	2	÷	12

2

1	×	6	=	6
=	32	÷	4	×
8	=	1	=	2
×	8	÷	8	=
4	=	3	÷	12

3

3	×	8	=	24
=	8	×	4	÷
5	=	4	=	6
÷	8	÷	32	=
40	=	10	×	4

4

72	÷	8	=	9
=	30	÷	6	×
5	=	35	=	2
×	7	×	5	=
6	=	3	÷	18

5

3	×	8	=	24
=	8	×	4	÷
5	=	4	=	6
÷	8	÷	32	=
40	=	10	×	4

ANSWERS

6

8	×	1	=	8
=	24	÷	4	÷
2	=	48	=	2
×	8	×	6	=
12	=	3	×	4

Unit 18

1. 28 ÷ 4 = 7
2. 36 ÷ 9 = 4
3. 54 ÷ 9 = 6
4. 81 ÷ 9 = 9
5. 48 ÷ 6 = 8
6. 36 ÷ 6 = 6
7. 56 ÷ 7 = 8
8. 27 ÷ 9 = 3
9. 63 ÷ 9 = 7
10. 49 ÷ 7 = 7
11. 49 ÷ 7 = 7
12. 72 ÷ 9 = 8
13. 63 ÷ 7 = 9
14. 54 ÷ 9 = 6
15. 64 ÷ 8 = 8

Unit 19

1. 10 ÷ 2 = 5
2. 6 × 2 = 12
3. 6 × 7 = 42
4. 12 ÷ 2 = 6
5. 15 ÷ 5 = 3
6. 9 ÷ 3 = 3
7. 3
8. 12
9. 2 12 3 8 4 6
10. 36 ÷ 9 = 4
11. 9 × 3 = 27
12. True
13. 9 ÷ 9 = 1
14. 1 2 3 4 6 12
15. 63

Unit 20

1. $4
2. $6
3. 42 chocolate drops, 28 chews, 63 dog biscuits
4. Clare by 8 points
5. Octopuses
6. $3 every 3 days for 8 weeks
7. $6
8. 16 packets with 3 in each
9. 8
10. 9

Test 1

1. 5 × 9 = 45
2. 5 × 7 = 35
3. 5 × 6 = 30
4. 10 × 6 = 60
5. 10 × 1 = 10
6. 10 × 7 = 70
7. 1 × 7 = 7
8. 0 × 6 = 0
9. 5 × 0 = 0
10. 2 × 8 = 16 2 × 16 = 32
11. 2 × 7 = 14 2 × 14 = 28
12. 6 × 4 = 24
13. 9 × 5 = 45
14. 9 × 6 = 54
15. 9 × 9 = 81
16. 9 × 5 = 45
17. 7 × 9 = 63
18. 8 × 9 = 72

Test 2

1. 8 × 5 = 40 5 × 8 = 40
2. 8 × 9 = 72 9 × 8 = 72
3. 7 × 7 = 49
4. 7 × 1 = 7
5. 7 × 4 = 28
6. 6 × 6 = 36
7. 6 × 9 = 54
8. 6 × 7 = 42
9. 48 = 6 × 8
10. 56 = 7 × 8
11. 81 = 9 × 9
12. 45 ÷ 9 = 5 9 × 5 = 45
13. 36 ÷ 4 = 9 4 × 9 = 36
14. 36 ÷ 6 = 6 6 × 6 = 36
15. 2 × 6 = 12 3 × 4 = 12

Back to Basics Multiplication Tables Years 4–5

Reprinted 2016, 2018

ISBN: 978 1 74215 935 5

Published by Pascal Press
PO Box 250
Glebe NSW 2037
www.pascalpress.com.au
contact@pascalpress.com.au

Author: Ann Baker
Publisher: Lynn Dickinson
Editor: Eliza Hope
Proofreader: Tim Learner
Design and illustration: Janice Bowles
Page layout and technical illustration: Ruth Schultz
Cover design: Deb Snibson, MAPG
Printed by Thumbprints